HOW DO YOU SAY, "I LOVE YOU"?

JUDSON J SWIHART

InterVarsity Press
Downers Grove
Illinois 60515

InterVarsity Press is the book-publishing division of Inter-Varsity Christian Fellowship, a student movement active on campus at hundreds of universities, colleges and schools of nursing. For information about local and regional activities, write IVCF, 233 Langdon St., Madison, WI 53703.

ISBN 0-87784-579-4
Library of Congress Catalog Card Number: 77-72524

Printed in the United States of America

17   16   15   14   13   12
91

To my wife, Nancy,
who through her gentle patience
has taught me much
about communicating love

Table of Contents

Preface

Many husbands and wives love each other, but they just cannot seem to get it across. Though they are loved, they do not feel loved. Why? Perhaps it is because they each talk a different language of love. Each one says, "I love you" and hears "I love you" in different ways, in ways the other does not understand.

This book explains why husbands and wives so often fail to communicate their love. Eight chapters consider eight languages of love, and show how they are used and abused. Chapter ten covers principles which apply to all languages of love and focuses on learning to speak the language your spouse understands. The final chapters are designed to help those who have tried to say "I love you" but have been resisted by their spouses. I hope, by all of this, not only to help readers understand the unique ways in which they now communicate but to encourage all married couples to say "I love you" in new and more effective ways.

Acknowledgments

Due to the nature of this manuscript, I thought it would be both useful and appropriate to obtain the critique of a psychologist, a marriage counselor, a theologian and a sociologist. I would like to thank the following friends for reviewing the manuscript for me. Charles Maxson, Dick and Dorothy Oldenburg, George Rekers, Art Sward, Phil Swihart and Don Tweedie. I would also like to thank Rita Teel for her insightful comments and assistance in typing the manuscript and Doris Ahl for assistance in typing the revisions of the manuscript.

1

A New Commandment

They sat side by side on the couch in my office, but they were on opposite sides of the earth. Their marriage of eighteen years was over. She had endured years of feeling unloved and had determined that she could no longer survive emotionally. She had been taking a long time to make a decision, and this process was now in its final stages.

"He doesn't love me. He never has and he never will." Her voice was bitter.

His reaction was shock and resignation: "How can you say that? I have done everything for you. I have provided well for you. I carry all the life insurance I can possibly handle. I've made excellent investments. If anything ever happened to me, you and the kids would be well provided for. Do you think that I would do that if I didn't love you?"

Obviously unimpressed she responded, "But you are never around when I need you. You are so preoccupied with your work that you hardly know I exist. Is that love?"

Starving for a more intimate relationship, for more time together, she was blinded by her own needs and unable to see his expression of love—providing material things for her. She didn't see his second job as a way of saying, "I love you," but rather as neglect of her and her needs. Money did not mean love to her.

What did he mean by love? How did he express it? What did she hear from his involvement in a second job?

A Dynamic Relationship

What is love? An emotional high? A commitment? A friendship? A significant experience with someone you are preoccupied with?

In this book I consider love in a broad sense. Love is more than an emotional high or a physiological response. Love involves commitment, respect, concern and a sense of union. In one study of love done with couples reporting a happy marriage, the couples defined love as a form of *relationship* rather than as a feeling, attitude or character trait.[1]

The Bible defines love by describing its dynamics. It is as though love cannot be defined apart from its expression.

Love is patient, love is kind. It does not envy, it does not boast, it is not proud. It is not rude, it is not self-seeking, it is not easily angered, it keeps no record of wrongs. Love does not delight in evil but rejoices in the truth. It always protects, always trusts, always hopes, always perseveres. (1 Cor. 13:4-7, NIV)

Although not everyone agrees on an exact definition of love, everyone agrees that the expression of love is an integral part of every vital marriage. Love is found in most marriages in one form or another—even if the marriage partners do not know how it is communicated in their relationship.

When do you feel loved? When does your spouse feel loved by you? Are you consciously aware of what forms of love expressions are received from you? Or are you like the wife in one research study who never noticed any change even when her husband, during a trial period, increased his affectionate responses. He said, "I love you," in ways which had meaning to him but which she did not hear.[2] Communication systems break down when husband and wife have chosen different "languages" and fail to communicate in a language which the other can understand.

"Ich Liebe Dich" en Français

Imagine for a moment a scene in a small village of France. It is a beautiful summer day and tourists are slowly roaming the streets. One of them is a handsome young German. As he approaches one of the shops, he sees a very attractive French girl. He decides that he would very much like to make her acquaintance as he watches her interacting with other customers. Obviously he does not love her since he does not know her, but he finds her very intriguing.

As he approaches the counter he begins to think about what he would like to say to start things off. After he has carefully chosen his words he speaks to her. She smiles at him with an inquiring look and nods her head. She does not understand German since she speaks only French. He is disappointed because his message was not clear to her; he has not been able to get to know her or to express himself. Since he speaks only German, she is not able to communicate with him either.

The same is true of the "languages" of love in marriage. Often the wife enters speaking French and the husband speaking German—in an emotional sense. Unless you hear love expressed in a language that you understand emotionally, it will have little value. There are a number of ways couples can communicate their feelings. It is the primary task of every marriage partner to discover the languages that are used and then to learn to effectively use these languages to communicate feelings and attitudes of love.

A middle-aged executive complained to me, "All my wife ever wants me to do is tell her that I love her. I feel that just saying the words doesn't mean a thing. It's actions that count."

On the other hand his wife said, "My husband is always bringing things to me to prove to me that he loves me. But he will never tell me so in words. How do I know what all of the gifts mean? I think he is trying to buy my love."

Obviously they are not speaking the same language. The husband is trying to show his love by giving things, but the wife cannot hear the love in the gifts. She wants

14

to hear the words from his lips. He feels that she is rejecting his love by not receiving his gifts with the right attitude. Consequently he feels hurt and rejected.

The reason this sort of situation is quite common is that most people only speak those languages they themselves are able to understand. They assume everyone else will understand the languages too. Because our middle-aged executive understands that love is expressed when gifts are given, he expects everyone else, including his wife, to understand as well. But making this assumption can be the first step in communication breakdown, and thus the potential for a love relationship will not be realized.

The Two Halves of Loving
From infancy through childhood we learn how to determine when someone loves us. Initially love comes from our parents or parent substitutes. It also comes from other members of the family and from those who are important or significant to our lives. After learning different things about expressing love, we begin to write our own definition or "language" of love, and it becomes an integral part of our personality. We have chosen one or more means of communication that we will value, accept and use as indications of love. We develop the yardstick which we will use to measure how much we are loved, particularly by our spouse, where this "need to know" seems most important. Why we constantly need to know how much we are loved, why we never seem to accept this once and for all, seems to be related to the fact that relationships are dynamic, rather than static. Whenever

15

we exist in a changing environment, we seem to feel a pressing need to monitor the changes as well as what remains the same. That requires constant checking and rechecking.

Interestingly and perhaps unfortunately we spend most of our time measuring how much we are loved rather than measuring how much we are loving. The more secure we become in a love relationship, the less we seem to measure.

Since we have each developed yardsticks for communicating love, we need to be aware of them to be certain they give us accurate readings—readings that measure what we want to measure, that are sensitive to the communicator's language. We can become confused by the ups and downs as we chart out our results. Sometimes we can even feel unloved. Occasionally we get unexpected measurements. These cause apprehension and in turn call for more measurements requiring more communication. These may help to clarify matters, but they may also confuse them if the communication is in a language that is foreign and not understood. Love expressed is not sufficient. It must be heard to have any meaning. If it lands on deaf ears, it is ineffective.

Communication is the product of an intricate process of selecting and sifting information and assigning it personal meaning.[3] We need to be aware of how we hear communication and be aware of our ability to express ourselves. Being a good transmitter is really what this book is all about—how to communicate love effectively, how to be aware of the languages your spouse speaks and then to communicate so he or she understands.

What happens when many of the greetings of love are filtered out, and one or both of the marital pair are not feeling loved? One of several avenues is available. Sometimes the spouse who is not feeling loved will give up and live in silent resentment. He or she may go years thinking this is his or her lot in life and will just bear with it. Others, not recognizing the role which their filter system has played will leave the marriage thinking, "If only I get a loving spouse, my feelings will be changed." They often enter another marriage only to find their same old filter system busy in that relationship too. There are still others who set about extracting the feeling they want from their spouse by playing such roles as the weak and helpless little girl, the seductive mistress or the big boss man.

Do manipulation and force work? Not really. For love should be the motivation behind the expression as well as the expression itself. The manipulated husband feels pressured, and the wife who is forced into subjection becomes resentful and rebellious. Both will tend to give less.

Let us forget the use of manipulation and force. But let us not give up. Instead, let us learn the primary language our spouse speaks and then communicate love in that language. Let us find ways to love that are meaningful and that are not filtered out quickly and easily because of past experiences.

Learning to Give Bread Not Stones
Individuals often marry someone very different from themselves. Therefore it is imperative that couples un-

derstand the confusion that can arise over the difference in the ways we say and hear, "I love you." With the principles you find in these pages I hope you will be able to speak in new languages to communicate effectively your feelings to others. The earlier you discover these keys the better chance your marriage has to develop the unity that God intended it to have.

I think of the expression, "What man of you, if his son asks him for bread, will give him a stone?" (Mt. 7:9). In some marriages husbands and wives are giving each other rocks instead of bread. As a result they are starving the relationship. We need to learn how to give each other the bread of love. Jesus gave us the standard for our love. "A new commandment I give to you, that you love one another; even as I have loved you, that you also love one another" (Jn. 13:34). There are many languages of love. Eight major ones are discussed in the following eight chapters.

2
Meeting Material Needs

In a society of affluence, where prestige and status are tied to possessions, we often associate the acquisition of luxury items with being loved. Somehow the *need* for a house gets translated into the *desire* for a better-than-average house. Few want to be seen driving an outdated car or dressed in anything other than the latest fashion. The pressure of providing for material desires has resulted in what we call the rat race—although we think little about the rats and greatly about the race!

The desire for things can become related to love. A husband who cannot bring himself to tell his wife the affection he feels may, instead, lavish her with gifts. What do gifts mean to her? And what message does she hear when the flow of gifts becomes only a trickle—or dries up entirely? If a strong association between gifts and love has been built in, her feelings of being loved will also dry up.

The husband we spoke of in chapter one, who had invested and purchased large sums of life insurance for his family, was using this language as a vehicle to communicate his love. Because this was what would make him feel loved, he assumed that everyone else would also feel loved when their physical needs were met.

In marriage, love seeks to discern the genuine needs of the loved one and meet them. A husband, for instance, would not express mature love by bringing home a pair of expensive earrings when what his wife needs is someone to mind the baby while she gets out with her lady friends one afternoon a week.[1]

This principle is seen in Don who had dreams of some day providing his wife, Alice, with a beautiful home, clothes and everything else she wanted. To be able to do this he worked both day and night. Always in the back of his mind was love for Alice and the need to provide tangible things to demonstrate his love. Meanwhile, at home she was struggling to raise three boys who desperately needed a father. Because providing for material desires was not her language, she could not understand his motivation. Consequently, she felt abandoned. As she began to express the need to have him home more, her husband felt unappreciated and overdemanded, and became resentful.

A Lonely, Blue Shirt
A number of years ago a couple came to see me. They

were pleasant and willing to bend and grow in order to enrich their marriage. As we explored their relationship one evening, we hit upon a subject that had been unresolved. Tom was irate. That morning as he was dressing for work he had reached into the closet for a shirt only to find there was no selection. One lonely, blue shirt greeted him. Anger welled up within him. Was this all that Ruth could do for him? Was this all that she cared? One blue shirt's worth? As he confronted her with his feelings of neglect, she was stunned. He knew that she had been particularly busy that week. The baby was sick. They had company for the weekend. Surely he could understand that she had not intentionally neglected his wardrobe. All communication broke down. Tom left for work with his blue shirt, feeling angry and frustrated. Ruth sat down and had a good cry, feeling unappreciated and misunderstood.

That evening as we explored his feelings, we found some clues to his behavior. As a child he had never been really sure that he was loved. He had decided that the best way to know how much he was loved was by how much his physical desires were met. This became his primary language. When his parents fed him well, gave him a bicycle, made sure he had new clothes, or gave him other things, he determined that he was loved. Therefore, unconsciously, he was using the same language as a barometer of her love. It was very painful for him to find only one or two shirts because of the message he heard in this. Seeing only one blue shirt in the closet was as though his wife were saying to him, "I really don't care much about you." Those painful feelings were unnecessary, for that was not her feeling at all. From her vantage point that one shirt meant, "I have been up all night with a sick baby who demanded my attention."

In the same way most of us, at one time or another, go through the same process of feeling hurt and angry because we have misread our spouse's message. Our spouse was not speaking our language, and we have misheard his or her attitude of love.

Another husband knew that his wife appreciated fine things. Tony had seen Kathy's face glow when she showed visitors around their lovely home, proud of the fine furnishings and tasteful decor. But he also knew that in order to maintain their standard of living he would have to continue his second job. This he was willing to do because he loved her and he wanted her to feel loved. Little did he realize how Kathy's filtering system was receiving this message.

"He is buying me off," she reasoned. "Rather than spending time with me he would rather work at a second job. He buys me all these things because he feels guilty about not spending more time with me." She was not hearing his language of love. It was being filtered out. She was dealing with it, but not in the way that he thought she was. Not only was his message unheard, it was reversed and seen as an expression of antagonism. It is not unusual for this particular language to have a detrimental effect if not heard precisely as intended.

The language of providing for material needs and desires can be especially meaningful when the giver sacrifices something of value to himself to provide for the need of the other. I think this is best illustrated in the well-known Christmas story of the wife who sold her hair to buy her husband a watch chain for the watch he valued so much. Unknown to her he had sold his watch to buy her an expensive barrette for her beautiful hair which she cherished.

This language has other forms as well. We may not desire food, clothing or other material possessions, but we may want our spouse to provide services for us. Joan and Ned had little in common. She was in the process of obtaining a divorce because of the emotional emptiness in their relationship. However, there was one bright spot in their otherwise deplete marriage. Joan had told me, "The one thing that he does that makes me happy is driving me to the doctor for my weekly treatment. It is the only time that I have any feelings for him." He was meeting a tangible desire. He was going out of his way to do it. She was responding because it was her language, and she could hear it when she heard little else.

A Child with Basic Needs

There are several reasons why people are led to use this particular language. One of our first experiences is to be provided for by our mother. This is one of the earliest and most basic expressions of love we experience. If our physical needs were not met adequately in infancy and early childhood, we will be especially sensitive to this language of love. It will be more important to us that those we love give to us and let us know that they desire to help meet our needs.

There are also children who have not been deprived of tangible needs but have grown up in homes where parents have given them many things as an outpouring of their love. As adults, these children will also tend to express their love for others by meeting their tangible needs and desires.

As a child, a girl is told she is loved mostly by having all tangible desires readily met. What happens to her when she marries while she and her husband are still students in college? There is little money. Yet she has brought into the relationship her concept of love being associated with receiving material things.

A number of everyday experiences fall into this category. First, there is the husband who likes to surprise his wife with occasional gifts. We all know the impact that flowers can have when brought home unexpectedly. In fact, this may be a good way for a husband to test his wife's use of this language. What does she do when you bring flowers? Does she feel loved or does she wonder what you have done wrong?

I find that wives more often go to extra effort in preparing a meal when they want to express affectionate feelings. They get the right cut of steak, add all the trimmings and set the atmosphere, maybe including music. If the husband speaks this language, he will feel loved. Fortunately for me, my wife Nan speaks this language with her baking. When she makes my favorite cookies (just because she knows I enjoy them), I get the message! She in turn enjoys my response of verbal appreciation, even though I spread crumbs all over the house.

The Bible has a number of examples of such love. Jacob loved Joseph and expressed it by presenting him with a beautiful multicolored coat. The message was so clear to the brothers that they were provoked to jealousy, envious of the special love relationship between their father and younger brother.

When Samuel went to live with Eli in the temple, his mother came to visit him each year. With each visit she would bring him a coat that she had made during the year. It was her way of trying to show him her love. Samuel must have wondered at times why she had left him with the old priest, perhaps wondering if she really did love him. Hannah, perhaps aware of his feelings, attempted to reassure him of her love with her annual gift.

Take a moment to reflect on how this language is expressed and heard in your own relationship. What tangible needs of your spouse do you seek to meet? Does he or she hear this language? What is the response?

3
Helping
Each Other

One of the spiritual gifts mentioned in the Bible is "helps." This is one of the languages of love many people can hear. We all appreciate a helping hand when the task seems heavy. How gratifying it can be to join together and tackle what might otherwise be an overwhelming task to carry out alone! Sharing work and looking forward together to a common goal can be very satisfying. The person bearing the primary responsibility for the task is likely to feel the love of the helper.

We have all heard the word *helpmates* referring to a husband/wife team. The problem is that many people spend ten per cent of the time thinking about being a helper and ninety per cent of the time thinking about being mates. Sometimes it is difficult to get out of that comfortable easy chair and abandon "Kojak" in the middle of a shoot-out to help your wife with the dishes, but the very fact that it is hard to do communicates love. Without being a sacrifice, helping would not have much meaning.

There are many different ways we can help each other. However, prior to launching an I-am-going-to-help campaign, we need to become aware of our spouse's goals, what his/her needs are and what tasks seem to be heavy to him/her. After we have determined where and when our help is needed, then we can roll up our sleeves and pitch in.

The Monthly Furniture Migration

Some friends of ours have different interests. Jerry basically likes indoor work and Judy likes to work outside. One of her hobbies is raising flowers. Like every gardener, Judy spends much of her time in weeding her flower beds—a monumental task to her. Her husband, who has little interest in flowers, will occasionally help her. He does this because he sees her face radiate as he sets about the task of uprooting those frustrating, little, old weeds.

For my wife and me it is different. Nan is a mover of furniture. I never know from one month to the next where I will find my favorite chair. One week it will be in the dining room, the next in the living room and the following in our bedroom. When she begins the monthly migration, she is on cloud nine if I help. She has a task she enjoys, and when I help with the heavy part, she feels like the most beloved lady in the land. Caring about what's important to Nan shows I care about Nan.

Expressing love in this language can be even more difficult and yet more effective late at night. To use this language means you can no longer wait for your spouse to get up when the clock says 3:00 A.M. and one of the children is crying. It means you no longer lie there pretending to be asleep, hoping your spouse will give way before you do.

The language of helping becomes more intense when the need for assistance becomes more acute. When your wife is sick and every effort to move is painful, there are still things to be done. She can greatly appreciate your stepping in at that time.

Early in our marriage we were bogged down and limited in our ability and willingness to help each other in some areas. Each of us had determined what jobs were fitting for a man in order to keep his male image and what tasks a woman was allowed to do and still retain her femininity. A typical scene would occur after dinner. Both of us had worked a full day on the job. Nan had come home early, picked up the newspapers, shoes and paraphernalia scattered around, and then prepared dinner. After the meal was over I would retire to the living room to read the paper, scattering more papers around the now tidy room, while Nan would be left in the kitchen alone, cleaning off the table and doing the dishes. Little did I realize that the resentment those dishes were done with was due to the lack of help and sensitivity on my part.

Nan was feeling neglected and used. She would have been delighted if I had stayed in the kitchen to help just a little, visiting and sharing in this menial task. Instead, from her viewpoint, I was taking advantage of her so I could have a quiet and relaxing time. She actually felt that if I loved her I would have wanted to stay in the kitchen until both of us had finished the work. After all, she had been working in a career world all day also.

I, on the other hand, had not even considered staying in the kitchen. I had determined that this was a job for women and sometimes kids—since I had washed many a plate and cup in my preadolescent years. Men, especially when women were around, *never* did dishes. That was strictly a woman's job. Unaware that it had even crossed Nan's mind, I was content in my easy chair doing what was proper for a man . . . in order to keep abreast of the world situation.

That was when we first got married. Today things have changed. I still seldom help specifically with the dishes when Nan is home, although I often do them if she is not there for a meal. However, now the help is there in another form. During the time allotted for cleaning up after the meal there are three small children who need food cleaned from their faces and clothing, and who need to be listened to (with the concentration of an athlete) as they tell the important events of the day, like the ladybug they were able to capture single-handedly. Then they must be prepared for bed. Nan is just grateful to be in her quiet kitchen, alone for a little while.

Overcoming Unnecessary Limitations
Sometimes roles also limit the expression of this language by a wife. Harry works in the city and returns home late in

the evening. There is very little time for him to do much around the house. Although he wants to keep the yard in tiptop shape, he just never seems to be able to find the time to get all the weeding, edging, raking and pruning done. All he can manage to do is to keep the lawn mowed. His wife, Louise, is "just a homemaker." Although she, too, appreciates a beautiful yard and actually has some time to work in it, she can never bring herself to go out to do anything. She has been taught that women do not work at such outdoor tasks. Afraid that the neighbors might see her raking leaves, mowing the yard and sweating, she stays inside and waits while the grass grows higher and higher.

To speak the helping language to each other effectively, we must be willing to forget ourselves and our preconceived ideas of what we should and should not do. We need to take a close look at our spouses to understand what they feel about what they are doing or what they need to be doing. We have an obligation to be willing to change our behavioral patterns in order to enhance our marriages.

The need for help is especially keen with the time pressures of today's world. This is even more true for the mothers of small children. What do you do if junior, who is supposed to be sleeping, refuses to cooperate and screams his lungs out during the time mother is preparing dinner? She feels as if she is letting her husband down if he is expecting a warm meal when he arrives; and she feels that she is neglecting the baby if she does not quiet and comfort him. If her husband is understanding when he arrives, does not condemn her, but offers to help, she

31

will undoubtedly feel his love. Immediately she will begin to lose her feelings of frustration. Feeling that she is no longer in her predicament alone, she can begin to think more clearly and to function more effectively. Instead of the responsibility resting solely on her shoulders, they will become helpmates.

Think over what your spouse needs, wants or delights in having help with. In what way could you help so he or she would sense your communication of love?

One caution: Don't help your spouse when he or she neither wants nor needs it. This is neither helpful nor loving; it's overindulgence. The message then is, "You're incapable" rather than "I love you." This is particularly important with a spouse who feels so inadequate that any task appears overwhelming. This spouse needs just enough help to see hope in his or her ability to complete the task. From there on the need is for encouragement and praise. It is important to remember that help is not taking over but rather assisting while he or she retains the primary responsibility for what is to be accomplished.

Time and Money
The Good Samaritan saw the needs of the man lying along the road, and he did not hesitate to help. His action cost him time and money. He gave both generously. He told the innkeeper to whom he took the injured man to take care of him. The Samaritan promised to repay whatever it cost.

The gift of his time was just as generous. Whenever I am going on a trip, I tend to value my time highly. I am not very open to being generous with it. I have a destination and desire to arrive on schedule. Yet the man from Samaria interrupted his plans in order to help. It was not as if he had nothing else pressing him.

There is one other factor that a friend of mine pointed out to me once in commenting on this parable. The road that ran from Jerusalem to Jericho was dangerous to travel alone because it was an ideal place for thieves to prey upon individuals. The Samaritan had the perfect excuse for not helping. "This man should have known better than to travel this road alone. He knew what could happen to him. It was by his own choice that he brought this problem upon himself. It's his own fault. Why should I help him?"

This parable gives us good reason to reflect on our own marriages. When we do help, do we do so with generosity or do we say, "I will do as little as possible; I will help only enough to get by, only when it is demanded of me"? Or do we excuse ourselves: "He's the one who decided to stay up late and watch that television movie. Why should I help him?" or "I could help her with the laundry but she is the one who decided to go shopping this afternoon. It's her own fault that she is behind in her work"? The language spoken in these ways and under these circumstances is not the language of love. Instead it is the language of withholding.

Christ must have had in mind open generosity (the offering of help when it is not demanded or deserved) when he terminated his Good Samaritan illustration by saying, "Go and do likewise."

4
Spending Time Together

Christic always took time for individuals. With all that he had to accomplish in the short period of his public ministry, he could well have felt pressure. He saw the needs of others you and I would have overlooked. He could have set up a lecture hall or a college in a city and taught thousands of people, but he chose not to do so. He could have created a healing center to handle the sick and diseased from across Palestine, but he chose not to do so. He spent time with his disciples and his friends. In the midst of a busy day, much to the chagrin of the disciples, he even had time for children.

To take time with someone is to say, "I value you. I value being with you. Even if I don't agree with your ideas, I know that they are valuable to you." One of our most important possessions in today's fast-paced society is time. How often have we heard, "My husband never has time for me. His job is so demanding right now."

Everyone Gets the Same Amount

Time is a limited commodity. Some may have an endless supply of money and others a mound of possessions. But everyone gets the same amount of time. And we are all challenged by how to spend it. Will we use it for our own pleasure or self-seeking? Will we spend it on nurturing old wounds? Will we use it constructively or destructively? Will we use any of it for anyone else?

Somehow we have convinced ourselves that we must do things in a hurry. We move as fast as we can because if we do not, we think the time is lost and gone forever.

This thinking is particularly disruptive in a husband/wife relationship. When couples rush their time together, they will never know each other well. Oh, they take time to talk . . . but only until the CBS special comes on or until he has to dash to a meeting or until she has to get ready for her Tupperware party. Time together is most useful when it is unhurried and unrushed.

Time spent together is closely related to the degree of marital satisfaction. Such is the conclusion reached in research among middle-class wives who were disillusioned with their marriages. The most prevalent complaint they had was the feeling of neglect because their husbands were gone much of the time.

Quantity and Quality

The amount of time logged with another person does not

in and of itself indicate the quality of relationship, but it has been used frequently as a measurement of love. Time together is a crucial ingredient if an in-depth relationship is going to develop.

Time together need not necessarily be spent only in talking. It may be spent just being together. I can think back to times on vacations when I enjoyed being with my wife, sharing the same experience yet talking little. We enjoyed the same rushing mountain stream and the solitude without constant discussion. One of my associates frequently takes walks with his wife. They enjoy equally their lengthy discussions and their silent times just being with each other. Being aware of the other's presence is often as meaningful as a verbal interchange. By the same token, it is possible to be involved in a verbal relationship and still not be spending time together.

The frequent marital complaint of wives, "You never spend time with me," is often refuted by the husband who describes times and places he was present. However, he fails to recognize his wife is trying to tell him that when he is present physically, he is absent emotionally.

Recently I was talking to a wife who felt very ignored because her husband was rarely home and, when he was there, he was in the garage working on his hobby. She had built up considerable resentment over the years because she felt ignored. The pain was particularly intense because it evoked a situation similar to what she had experienced with her father who also was seldom home. Because of her background, spending time together was a very important language to her. No matter what other ways her husband attempted to communicate love, she

37

could not hear them and felt very unloved.

Some couples are sold on the idea that they do not need quantity time together. They only need quality time. I have yet to discover a way for a relationship to grow without a couple spending a significant amount of time together. The point is that quality and quantity are equally important; they are not to be substituted for one another. A relationship will not grow in love if that time is spent in critical and hostile exchanges, or if it is devoid of significant discussion. Likewise a relationship will not grow in love if the couple has only brief exchanges of meaningful thoughts and feelings.

Ordering Your Values

Any significant time *together* will involve unity and relationship, not just sharing the same room or general proximity. Nan and I have become sensitive to this language in our own marriage. I found myself trying to use Saturday as an additional time to be home. The only problem was that that time was also shared with the kids and the football games. Nan tried to talk to me and would sometimes get a "huh." Even half time was hectic because I used this time for a reconnaissance mission to the refrigerator. After I watched "the game of the century" for three consecutive Saturdays, Nan's patience and understanding were beginning to be as depleted as the refrigerator shelves. Since then, we have been able to work out a schedule in which we really do spend time together.

It is the responsibility of each spouse to re-evaluate his or her value system and to realize the importance of spending time together. For some this is the only way they will ever feel loved and valuable. As J. Allen Peterson has emphasized in his Family Life Conferences, "It is critical that we stop doing the things that are urgent and start doing the things that are important."

It is easy to ascertain where the husband is arranged in the value hierarchy of the wife by observing what she does for and with him. A wife who chooses to spend her time grading papers when her husband would like to talk, take a drive, or have intercourse and who says that she values her husband over her school work is deceiving herself.

In the same way a husband often deceives himself about the hierarchical value placement of his job and wife. Many husbands love their wives so much that they work at the office every night. Other husbands love their wives so much that they take their vacations without them and often with a mistress.[1]

Husbands, do you want to see if your wife can hear the language of spending time together? Call her and tell her you will be home early from work because you want to be with her. Then note her response. Or if you want to do it up big, offer to take her away for the weekend without the kids. I have seen marriages take on new dimensions because the couples routinely took time to go away for weekends together. The importance of this language of love should not be minimized. It often reveals what we really count as valuable.

5
Meeting
Emotional Needs

Emotional openness and responsiveness are two parts of the same language. To meet another's emotional needs, it is almost impossible not to have both. To be open, honest and vulnerable with another is to be responsive to his or her emotional needs. Likewise, being responsive to emotional needs requires some vulnerability on the part of the one who is reaching out. Openness and responsiveness thus represent key girders for building a solid relationship.

Meeting each other's emotional needs is not always simple. Several factors should be mentioned before discussing just how we can speak this language of love. First, as mentioned before, emotional development begins at birth. We experience fear, jealousy, anger, sadness, joy, elation, happiness. Some of our emotional needs in child-hood are met and some are not. Often the pattern that develops carries on into adult life and marriage. Many studies conducted regarding unmet needs tend to center around the "inner child" (which remains part of us throughout life) and its needs for loving affirmation.[1] Thus emotional needs vary from person to person depending on background as well as on circumstances and character.

Because our needs vary, it is important not to assume that your spouse has exactly the same emotional needs that you do. Most likely he or she does not. According to some studies the husband and wife are markedly different in their emotional make-ups in as many as seventy per cent of marriages. For example, Paul Tournier has expressed a common, though generalized, difference between the communication systems used by husband and wife:

> *Speech itself has a different meaning for men than it has for women. Through speech men express ideas and communicate information. Women speak in order to express feelings, emotions. This explains why a wife will relate ten times an experience she has lived. It is not to inform her husband. He cuts her off sharply, "I know it already; you've told it to me before." But she needs to tell it again in order to discharge emotional tension which the experience has built up in her heart.*[2]

Second, we are naturally protective of ourselves, naturally defensive. We find it hard to reach out to others because of the need to protect our own emotions and our strength from harm.

42

Each one speaks primarily in order to set forth his own ideas, in order to justify himself, in order to enhance himself and to accuse others. Exceedingly few exchanges of viewpoints manifest a real desire to understand the other person.[3]

I will say more about this later in the chapter.

Third, emotions may seem to be far more trouble than they are worth. But we need to remember that emotions are a gift from God. We were created as emotional beings. The Fall has made us prone to distort or misread our emotions, just as it has distorted every aspect of who we are. It has made our emotions imperfect. But condemning them, neglecting them or pretending they are not there is no solution. For better or worse our emotions are an important part of us. Whether they are better or worse depends upon how we use them.

Love Is Listening

The place to begin, then, in meeting emotional needs is to determine what those needs are. The very attempt itself is a powerful expression of love. And when the attempt succeeds, the results are even stronger. Virtually every time a person feels understood, feels that his spouse understands his emotional needs, he will also feel loved. "Communication is at its best when two people mutually serve one another in love, each reaching out to the need of the other."[4]

Recently a wife told me, "I only wish my husband would respond to me." Tom did not know what to do with Sandy's emotional needs. So he just froze up and ignored them. When she expressed her feelings, Tom did not comment. His lack of involvement meant, "I don't know

43

how to help you." But she heard, "I don't care that you are hurting." Of course that meant, "I don't care about you." It was difficult for Sandy because now in addition to her hurt, she was also trying to deal with her feelings about what she thought was Tom's lack of caring. How much better are those marriages in which a wife expresses some feeling of pain and the husband empathizes. The wife gains comfort from feeling that her husband is involved with her.

Seeking to understand one's spouse requires taking time to hear, to ask, to observe or communicate in a language that is understood. It takes effort. Paul Tillich has said, "Love that cares, listens."[5] Anyone who has concentrated on listening to another knows it is work. But it can be the most powerful action in showing acceptance of another person.[6]

To be a good listener one must practice.

In order to really understand, we need to listen, not reply. We need to listen long and attentively. In order to help anybody to open his heart we have to give him time, asking only a few questions, as carefully as possible in order to help him better explain his experience.[7]

Good listening involves tuning in the other person. This means listening intently rather than waiting to get a word in edgewise or thinking of other events and people. How often have we cut off communication by completing sentences for our spouse, interrupting with wisdom or advice, looking away or becoming distracted? To listen involves giving undivided attention to the one who is speaking. The Bible encourages us in James 1:19, "Let every man be swift to hear, slow to speak and slow to wrath."

To really listen by posture, attention and words is to say, "What you have to say is important," and this is often translated, "You are important." Listening creates the atmosphere for the other person to begin to experiment with unmasking himself. When unmasking begins, we begin to learn the other's needs. Thus listening helps us know the person rather than simply know about him.[8]

Knowing and Opening

Being known and being vulnerable involve very similar concepts. It is difficult to have one without the other. In *Why Am I Afraid to Tell You Who I Am* the answer given to the book's title is, "If I tell you who I am, you may not like who I am, and it is all that I have." Being understood means becoming vulnerable. Whenever you open up yourself to being known by your spouse, you run the risk of being hurt or rejected. But you also open up yourself to the possibility of a loving relationship. You must be able to take the risk of revealing who you are, what you think, feel and value.

Christ was vulnerable and sensitive to others' feelings. When he saw Mary and Martha hurting because of Lazarus's death, he wept with them. The Jews thought he was weeping because of his love for Lazarus. Although it is not stated specifically, I believe Christ was also moved by compassion because of his sensitivity to the painful loss of his friends Mary and Martha. His openness to others created his vulnerability. They also found out more about Jesus.

Expressing your innermost feelings to your spouse shows love through vulnerability. It is saying, "I want you

45

to know me and to be a part of me. To do this I am letting you know how I feel." The concept of two becoming one flesh can only be achieved if husband and wife know each other intimately. A spouse who does open himself up to the other becomes vulnerable to being judged or criticized. Because of this, it is hoped that both will sense the trust that they have in each other.

A husband and wife may know a great deal of information about each other without really knowing each other. To know each other is to know the meaning of each other's life and not just each other's history.[8]

I recall talking to a rather insightful wife who in the process of counseling became aware of this in her marriage. She said rather slowly and with some degree of amazement, "After twenty years of marriage, I don't even know him." They had gone years without disclosing themselves to each other. Years went by without their really feeling loved.

Of all the arguments against love none makes so strong an appeal to my nature as, "Be careful! This might lead you to suffering." There is no "safe" investment. To love at all is to be vulnerable.

Letting the Drawbridge Down

Loneliness is the price for protection. Some people are like medieval castles. Their high walls keep them safe from being hurt. They protect themselves emotionally by permitting no exchange of feelings with others. No one can enter. They are secure from attack. However, inspection of the occupant finds him or her lonely, rattling around his castle alone. The castle dweller is a self-made prisoner. He or she needs to feel loved by someone, but the walls are so high that it is difficult to reach out or for anyone else to reach in.

What is the solution? There has been a rather unhealthy movement of late that encourages people to tear down all their walls. I find that people cannot remain totally defenseless for very long. There is, however, another option. A person can sometimes put a drawbridge in the castle wall. When someone makes the effort to truly understand him, the bridge may be lowered so that friends can come in to share his inner life.

It is necessary to have some openness if we ever expect to achieve our emotional potential in life. If we choose never to come out from our defenses, we will have missed part of the essence of life itself.

It is important, however, not to depend on our marriage partner for total understanding every time we have a need. Unfortunately, no matter how we think in heavenly terms, we end up married to a mortal. Some may enter marriage with unrealistically high expectations for being understood. We dreamed that there was someone out there who was to be our knight in shining armor or our ladylove. With this person we would be able to experience the freedom to be ourselves without ever being misunderstood again.

My wife's secret ambition was to find the person described by Emerson: "My friend is a person with whom I may be sincere. My friend does not cause me to stoop, to lisp or to mask myself." And then, the day came. We said our vows and began our magical experience . . . except reality soon set in, and we found that in self-defense our masks were sometimes back in place protecting us from the one who was to be our understanding friend.

Part of your concept of your mate will change as you get to know and understand him or her. Your spouse may not live up to your expectations. Yet you need to know him. If you have ever noticed your spouse with his or her castle walls up, this is your signal that it is time for understanding. It is not a time for a frontal attack on his or her defenses nor a time for beginning a little castle construction yourself.

What does meeting emotional needs of your spouse mean on a daily level? Well, it varies considerably from one person to another. Dobson in *What Wives Wish Their Husbands Knew about Women* shows the tremendous emotional need of wives for self-esteem. For some couples it may mean providing security or stability in the marriage. Or it may be more antagonistic like the opportunity to be angry at your spouse without his or her being crushed or defensive. The daily needs are as unique to the person as their own personality is unique to them. The important thing is that you know them well enough to be able to utilize this language.

Here are some questions you may want to answer in writing. Doing this may help you speak the language of meeting emotional needs more fluently: What does your spouse need from you? Do you know your mate's most important emotional need? What makes the masks come back? What makes understanding and being understood so difficult? How can you communicate so this language of meeting emotional needs will be effective?

6
Saying
It with Words

The Bible tells us some interesting things about the power of the spoken word. Proverbs 15:4 and 18:21 claim that words can instill a sense of life. James 3:4-5 compares the tongue to the small rudder able to turn a great ship. Tremendous power is contained in verbal expression.

The Song of Solomon overflows with the author's verbal outpouring of love. His efforts to express himself result in phrases like, "Thy love is better than wine," "Thy name is an ointment poured forth," "O thou fairest among women," and "As a lily among thorns so is my love." On and on in beautiful poetry he verbally expresses what he feels on the inside. It floods outward as though he cannot quite fully express his inner emotions.

Ten Times a Day

I have seen few marriage manuals which do not encourage the verbal expression of love as a routine part of any marriage. "I love you" or "I care" has great meaning to many husbands and wives. It is a language they hear. I am sure that you can think of many who grasp onto those words because they warm their inner being. They respond and accept them. They hear and consequently feel.

Verbal communication can be the most precise form of communication when used appropriately. It has as much precision as the speaker has self-awareness, self-honesty and clarity in presenting his or her ideas or feelings. In fact, the verbal can be used to clarify the non-verbal messages a spouse receives through the behavior of his or her mate. When a wife asks her husband for two months to fix a broken chair and there is no response, does it mean he does not care about her feelings? It could mean that. It could also mean many other things such as, "I feel a need to do other tasks," "I am angry at you," "I am afraid you'll criticize whatever I do," "I feel incompetent and am afraid I'll fail" or "I didn't realize it was that important to you."

How to resolve this situation? Words—not threatening, not accusing, but sincerely inquiring—can often get the exact message across.

Some husbands and wives want to accept the affectionate messages, "I care; I appreciate you," but they are hesitant to do so. They pretend not to accept verbal expressions, yet inside they ask themselves if they dare place value and meaning on that which is said. They would, in fact, be disappointed if the words ever stopped, even though they struggle to accept them fully.

A wife loves to hear her husband tell her over and over of his appreciation and love for her. Sometimes the husband, who may use communication mostly to convey information, assumes she already knows of his love. He has told her ten times. Why should he say it again? It is only repetitious. For her he could say it ten times every day and she would still face the next day waiting to hear it ten more times.

I have been both refreshed and delighted to watch the openness and trust shown by one of our close friends. She so readily accepts what is told to her that she sometimes embarrasses herself by naively accepting as fact things told to her that were illustrations or jokes. She takes them at face value. Though she is slightly vulnerable at this point, she also opens herself to a whole world of warmth because she can so fully hear her husband's verbal expressions of love and appreciation for her.

For others, words mean nothing. This is true of those who grew up in homes where people were intentionally or possibly unintentionally dishonest with their verbal communication. A person could not disclose what he really felt. One could say the right thing but not dare express the real feeling. Because of this background it is difficult for them to put much stock in this very verbal language of love. For them the lesson learned early was, "You really can't rely on what people tell you." You must use another yardstick if you are going to find out what someone is really thinking or feeling.

I previously mentioned a husband whose wife frequently wanted to be told that she was loved. He refused to do so because, as he explained to me, "Words mean absolutely nothing. It's the actions that count." His refusal, however, was related to more than just an intellectual protest. As a child he had often been encouraged and even coerced into verbal expressions of love toward his own mother. Now his wife, expressing her need for verbal reassurance only created resistance in him, in protest to being forced or requested to verbally express love.

We need to be sensitive to our spouses. Whenever we see resistance to some form of affectionate expression, their hesitancy may not necessarily mean that they do not love us. It may mean that they have had some difficult and painful experience with this language in the past.

When the Meatloaf Tastes Terrible

Honesty is the key to enhancing the effectiveness of the verbal communication—honesty with ourselves and our spouses. If we fool ourselves or don't seek to discover our true feelings, we can simply end up communicating our own self-deception. Or when a husband has for years told his wife what he thought she wanted to hear or whatever would not hurt her feelings, it becomes difficult for her to trust him when he does tell her how he truly feels. If you both know the meatloaf tastes terrible, it doesn't help the verbal language of love to brag about how wonderful it tastes.

Verbal expression must certainly be considered in the context of other forms of communication. There are times when verbally expressing love may be very effective and other times when the words will not be as meaningful. If your spouse's attention is focused on something that is important to him or her, that is not the time to expect your mate to be thrilled about the feelings you have expressed.

Tone and attitude are also to be considered. You can strengthen the effect of what is said or you can erase the effect by these things. The husband who blankly says to his wife, "I love you," while his eyes are fixed on the football game will hardly communicate sincerity. To be effective our *form* of expression needs to coincide with what is actually said.

The last point to consider is to make sure we express love with words only for the purpose of expressing love. Otherwise, one might question the motivation behind the message rather than listen to the message itself. When it is used to get something you want or to ward off anger, it detracts from its effectiveness. When the wife greets her husband at the door with, "Honey, I love you," it may raise his suspicions of her having forgotten to mail that important letter. Or he may wonder if he is about to learn that three days ago he was to call his boss back right away.

Sometimes spouses who are creative will verbally express their love through poetry. Using this creative format can make the impact greater and can help the language be heard more clearly. I recognize that not everyone has the ability to be a poet or even to think of a line that rhymes with "Roses are red, violets are blue." For the nonpoets, the hard work has been done. If your spouse appreciates love poems and you are looking for a creative way to express your feelings to him or her, it is always possible to find books of poetry in every bookstore. Certainly not all of us can, or even desire, to communicate our love through poetry. But if your spouse is sensitive to this verbal language, a simple verbal expression can be a powerful influence in your marriage.

Expressing love with words is not a one-way street. It needs to be a complete circuit. The sender is also responsible for making sure that his message got through and arrived intact. "I really care about you," may produce different reactions in husband and wife. One may have grown up in a family where *care* meant others encouraged them, supported them and helped them to be themselves. The other may have grown up in a family where parents kept them dependent, overprotected and emotionally bound to themselves because they "cared so much." As with the other languages of love, verbal expression needs to be constantly monitored to be sure the message gets through.

7
Saying It with Touch

Touching is the coup de grâce of communications. If one views man as a spiritual, emotional and physical being, he can appreciate the magnitude of this expression. Touching is the one communication form that allows a couple to be drawn into a spiritual, emotional and physical union of love all at the same time.

Because we are in part physical beings, we need to relate to our world through touch from the time of birth. For infants the need for touch is so great that they literally cannot survive without it. Through this sense mechanism early feelings of warmth, security and comfort begin to grow. Children thrive on this physical expression of love. When Christ wanted to communicate his love to them, he took them in his lap and held them in his arms.

The physical expression of love takes many forms, including touching, holding, sexual behavior, eye contact and positioning (for example, sitting close together on the couch while watching television or talking). As adults, we have a tendency to use this language in a more restricted capacity. As we mature, other forms of expression are available to us that were not as accessible in earlier years. It would be difficult for a child to express love by a predetermined plan to assist others in the development of their strengths or by trying to fully understand their emotional needs. So the older we get, the more we tend to communicate in ways in addition to touching or hugging. We also become more aware of what being touched means to others. We recognize that touching may be misinterpreted. The other person may feel an invasion of privacy. Hence, we become more cautious in our use of this communication form and less free in expressing it. Even within the marriage relationship we develop feelings about the social standards and timing of the expression. A wife may feel loved if her husband kisses her in their home but only feel self-conscious or embarrassed if he kisses her in the supermarket.

Recently, we have been deluged with literature on the importance of becoming aware of bodies as part of total self-awareness. We've also been informed on how we use our bodies to communicate with others. This whole area has developed into what we call the study of "body language." The focus is on what your body says. Does it reinforce other forms of communication, or does it tell your spouse a different message? It discusses how we can express ourselves without uttering a word. These issues and others are all a part of learning to use physical expression as a communication form.

For some, this language is very important if they are to hear the love their partners express. "The language of the body has a quality of unmatched validity. Words, on the contrary, lend themselves to easy corruption."[1] In some instances the physical seems to be a vehicle that can go beyond words or be used when the words just do not seem to come out because of intense emotions. When the prodigal son finally returned home, his father threw his arms around his son and kissed him to express what he was feeling inside.

In thinking about the physical expression of love there are many forms to consider. The message, "I love you," may be expressed by the warm embrace for the wife who feels tired from a long day of coping with children or a difficult day at her office. Sometimes a walk in the evening, hands interlocked, brings a sense of companionship. The playful pinch or the quick pat while passing in the hall can spark a feeling of mischievousness. It is all a recognition of the physical presence of someone who cares. For one wife greeting her husband at the door with a kiss may be an important expression of her love; for another a hand on his shoulder while pouring a second cup of coffee may tell of her desire to make contact with him emotionally as well as physically. These physical contacts say, "I am aware of you as a person, and I care about you."

The sexual expression of love is certainly an important part of this language. It is a form that can bring an indescribable oneness into a relationship. "One of the most significant things to say about sexual intercourse is that it provides husband and wife with a language which cannot be matched by any other act whatsoever. Love needs language for its adequate expression and sex has its own syntax."[2]

When husbands express love physically only through sexual behavior, the wife does not hear this message. She says to herself, "He is not loving me. He only wants to bring himself pleasure. He only pays physical attention to me when he wants to have sex." Some husbands are shocked to discover their wives feeling used, not loved.

For the sexual relationship to be meaningful, it must reflect true feelings of love. Where it is used for self, it becomes a ritualistic duty or a performance. The meaning is lost. It is said that Dr. Jung's comment on this was that sexual unhappiness is the result of having no love, only sexuality. When this happens, the language of touching is there in form, but the communication is gone. However, when the feeling is there as well as the form, its message and expression are beautiful. "Rejoice with the wife of your youth. As a lovely hind, a graceful doe, let her breasts satisfy thee at all times; be exhilarated always with her love" (Prov. 5:18-19, NASB).

The physical expression only mirrors what exists on the inside. I view with awe the ability we have been given. We are able to orchestrate a biological system of cells and tissues, combine it with an act of our will, and use this to express to our spouse feelings that exist in our innermost being. We are able to take the intangible and express it through the living and breathing.

8
Being on
the Same Side

I am particularly struck by God's Word that
"I will never fail you nor forsake you" (Heb. 13:5). I know
he is always there. He is always on my side, no matter
how badly I offend him, no matter how badly I fail. The
reassurance pours forth from the Scriptures. "If we are
faithless, he remains faithful—for he cannot deny himself" (2 Tim. 2:13). "We have an advocate with the
Father" (1 Jn. 2:1). Because he loves us he is our ally.

We all know how it feels to have someone who is "on
our side" when it seems we face the battle alone. Feeling
loyalty from your husband or wife is an important part of
every family. This does not mean he or she will always
agree with you but that your mate will always defend your
right to be yourself. And sometimes he or she may even

agree with your ideas and offer supportive information and arguments.

Faithfulness and Protection

This alliance seems to take on two primary forms. The first tells us that we can never do anything so negative that our husband or wife will not be for us. It is tremendous to know that your husband will be on your team— whether he agrees or disagrees with you. Sometimes you may not feel that he is, for instance, when you come home with a crumpled fender because you were checking your hair while backing out of the parking lot. Your husband may be angry about the fender as it relates to the $100.00 deductible insurance policy, but you know that he still values you above the fender. Your best interests are still his major concern. He can forgive because as a team member, he can identify enough with you to see the accident through your eyes. He is pulling for you emotionally because he is your ally.

The second form is protection. When I think of nations that are allies, I think of them as being on the same team; and I also think of defense or assistance with protection when battles are to be fought. This defending may mean defending from others or even from one's own weaknesses. It includes being an ally when one's spouse is being verbally assaulted by someone else. This is not to say that one could not be overprotected or protected when he does not need it. Because a good ally cares about the well-being of his comrade, he does not destroy him or her by overprotection. To do so would make their alliance less than what it was intended to be. An ally's motivation should be the protection of the other and the protection of his own ego or well-being. As with the other languages of love, misspeaking it can be as disruptive as not speaking it at all.

Allies in Public

How often we have seen the look on a wife's face when her husband does not act as her ally in public—and in fact berates her! A public attack by the one you thought was your ally is even more painful than a cutting remark in private. In this situation the wife has to deal with what the onlookers might think as well as with her husband's attitude. How this contrasts to the wife whose husband allies himself and uplifts her publicly by his comments!

Sue had several older brothers. Their frequent teasing generated a good deal of hostility within her. After she got married, her brothers would occasionally revert to their old behavior during visits together (although it was not nearly as caustic as before and was done in good humor). On these occasions Ted, her husband, not recognizing her feelings, would join in with them in what he saw as socially acceptable humor. It was not until after Ted became aware of the pain that this caused and changed his behavior to one of becoming her ally, that she was able to feel his love for her. Before this Sue felt he was not on her team, especially when the chips were down.

Sometimes the alliance is expressed in dealing with a difficult relative or in-law. We talk about the importance of a husband and wife leaving their parents and cleaving to each other. Their unity can be greatly enhanced when all in-laws understand that cleaving involves changing alliances from parents to one's spouse. When a wife or husband tries to keep parents as allies rather than transferring this to his or her spouse, it becomes divisive. It pulls couples apart. The in-laws can be very helpful at this point by relinquishing the alliance with their child and creating a new alliance between themselves as a couple and the new couple. It is a matter of communicating to the couple, "We are for you as a team" not "We will always stick up for you and defend you from that beast you were so unfortunate to marry."

My own parents were very helpful to me in making this adjustment in the early days of our marriage. Whenever, on behalf of the two of us, I would with great enthusiasm begin to formulate plans for an activity with them, I was gently asked to consider Nan's feelings and her plans for us. Their message was a clear reminder that, although they valued a shared activity, there were now two of us and our relationship together came before anything else.

Protection from Weakness
Being allies includes protecting each other from each other's weaknesses. Each spouse depends on the other's assistance. There are times when you may need an ally to protect you from yourself. It is like the Pogo comic that says, "We have met the enemy and he is us."

Being on the team is the wife who flags down her impulsive husband from overcharging their Bank Americard. She is saying, "On our team and as your ally I can complement you and save us disappointment later on."

It takes a husband with concern for and involvement with his wife to help her sort out priorities and prevent over-commitment in various activities because she has trouble saying "no." A good ally will face us with protective concern even though he or she may take flak from us for it. The message of "I care for you and am on your team" is felt when we realize the motivation behind the behavior. That motivation says, "I care about your well-being. I love you."

9
Bringing Out the Best

Last summer on vacation we had the privilege of visiting my cousin and his family on their walnut ranch in northern California. As we walked through the rich soil and neatly aligned row upon row of trees, he explained to us some interesting aspects of growing his crop. First, he had carefully selected the area. He had to find rich soil and a desirable climate so his trees would grow and prosper. Second, he and his family had worked several years in caring for and nurturing the trees. To this point they had still not received a crop of walnuts in return. He recognized that it took time, work and patient care before they would ever see any fruit from their labors. Although years had gone into his grove without any fruit, he remained involved and undaunted in his efforts, knowing that eventually the crop would come.

Greenhouse or Desert?
One of the greatest pleasures in marriage can be helping your spouse to reach the maximum of his or her potential. Your spouse's gifts are different from yours. His or her abilities and strengths are different from yours. As you recognize the importance of these and help your husband or wife grow, you are speaking love.

When I think of helping Nan to be all she can be, I think of my cousin's walnut ranch. What kind of climate and environment do we have in our home? Is it a climate in which Nan can grow as a person, where she can stretch to reach her potential?

Some homes and marriages are greenhouses where personal growth is marked and pronounced. Others are deserts in which there is no fruit. The individual's capacity shrivels and struggles to barely stay alive. Where are you living? Is the soil and climate rich, producing growth, or are you living in a desert, barely existing? Are you willing to spend years of work and patient caring to bring growth to your spouse? So often after a few weeks of trying to encourage our spouse, we see no crop, no fruit and give up, saying, "What's the use? My efforts are futile." My cousin did not hold any such unrealistic expectations.

It has been said that a fulfilled marriage can come only when each partner grows because of the union, rather than being slowly and surely squelched by it. The importance of helping one of the marriage partners to develop fully is not seen only in what this does for the individual. It affects the whole relationship. One person's gain or loss must have bearing on the total relationship. The potential for growth that lies within both husband and wife needs encouragement for the marriage to blossom.

What I am at any given moment is determined to a great extent by my relationships with those who love me or refuse to love me, with those whom I love or refuse to love.[1] We wield a great deal of influence with our spouses and therefore need in love to be sensitive to what we are doing with this power. We can provide the support and climate for growth to occur. The power to grow and the responsibility for the growth belong to the person himself. You cannot make another person feel satisfied, happy or more fulfilled. But you can commit yourself to assisting him, caring for him, not holding him back from reaching for those things in life that are meaningful.

The Price of a Xerox Copy

Several problems can keep this language from being spoken. The language encouraging potential will not be spoken where insecurity reigns. When the husband is not secure, he is threatened to see his wife develop and mature. He becomes fearful that she will outgrow him and find that she is bored and unsatisfied with him.

The problem comes into focus when the wife feels repressed and caged in because her husband fights her growth. She is forced either to rebel or to give in and accept her fate. If he increases his control, the marriage could eventually break under the pressure. If in the beginning the two had been able to encourage and support each other in their growth, the relationship would not have ended in a power struggle.

An insecure husband prefers his wife to be a copy of himself rather than to have her own personality. He gains security, but the price tag is high in what it does to their relationship. One is not emotionally, spiritually or intellectually stimulated by a Xerox copy of himself.

Selfishness is another factor that represses the language of encouraging potential. A husband or wife is focused on his own development so much that he puts no investment in helping his or her spouse. I think of a business associate of mine who has become so enmeshed in his profession that his wife has drifted into her own world marked by stagnancy. When I see her she does not look nor sound satisfied with her position in life. A walnut tree trying to grow in the desert?

A 1974 study found that one factor behind the love relationships of happily married couples was the attempts of each partner to balance the other's twin needs of individuality and intimacy.[2] They were helping each other achieve individual growth, yet they reserved some energy to dedicate to their own growth. Because you assist your spouse in helping him or her toward fulfillment does not mean that you must become stagnant.

Prayers and Praise

What is included in speaking this language in your home? For instance, when was the last time you brought your wife or husband materials for those special projects she or he likes to do? Perhaps you never thought of expressing your love through buying a ten-pound box of plaster of Paris. If your spouse is into making objects to paint, she or he may really respond to your thoughtfulness.

One husband told me, "I feel loved when my wife buys me a new saw for my workshop." He was a home carpenter and prided himself on the things he built for the home. A new saw helped him express himself with the skills he enjoyed.

Lastly, we cannot ignore spiritual development. When was the last time you thought of praying for your spouse? We know Christ and the apostles emphasized discipleship, but we forget that it applies to our spouse. Have you taken time to carefully consider discipling or building up your spouse? Here I am not thinking of a program in which you look down on your spouse with the idea of bringing him or her up to your level out of the goodness of your heart. Rather I am thinking of a conscientious sharing to maximize growth.

Paul gave us a good example of this in his relationship to the Christians in Thessalonica.

We give thanks to God always for you all, constantly mentioning you in our prayers, remembering before our God and Father your work of faith and labor of love and steadfastness of hope in our Lord Jesus Christ. . . . You became imitators of us and of the Lord, for you received the word in much affliction, with joy inspired by the Holy Spirit, so that you became an example to all the believers in Macedonia and Achaia. . . . We were gentle among you like a nurse taking care of her children. So being affectionately desirous of you, we were ready to share with you not only the gospel of God but also our own selves, because you had be-

come dear to us. (1 Thess. 1:2-3, 6-7; 2:7-8)
Paul prayed for the Thessalonians and worked with them
so that their faith became famous throughout Greece. He
praised them as well for the strides they had made. He
loved them, and he showed his love by helping them to
grow in the gospel of Christ and by giving of himself.

Through prayer for your spouse, he or she will grow
and feel cared for and loved because of your efforts and
faith. Do you know what your spouse could use prayer
for so that he or she might grow more in Christ? For me
this means praying for Nan to be less apprehensive when
she sings in front of audiences. It means praying that we
can afford that new dress or coat next month. These are
things that are important to her, even if they do not seem
of worldwide importance to me.

Let me close then with this encouragement from Paul:
"Do not let any unwholesome talk come out of your
mouths, but only what is helpful for building others up
according to their needs, that it may benefit those who
listen" (Eph. 4:29, NIV).

10
Principles
of Communication

Now that we have examined some ways to communicate affection, we are ready to consider some principles in the dynamic use of the languages. These principles apply to all marriages; though I recognize that some will apply more than others, depending on the couple. They will, however, offer a format for examining the languages used in your own marriage as well as a format for the application of the languages discussed in chapters two through nine. Most of these principles have been mentioned or implied previously. But it is important here to state them explicitly in review.

Principle 1: Remember It Is Filtered
"I get up every day and go to work whether I feel like it or

not. Even if I am sick. Now doesn't that say to my wife that I love her?" But his wife readily admits that she doesn't feel loved by him.

Often we glibly assume that what we have communicated has been received. Why do we never take the time to ask ourselves whether that message has in fact been received or filtered? We should never forget that all incoming information is screened and sifted. Sometimes we give mental assent to the cliché that people hear what they want to hear. But it needs to be emphasized that all incoming data is filtered to some degree. Why is this so? We cannot handle all the stimuli our society bombards us with. It is very demanding to try to evaluate each piece of information we encounter, so we form habitual patterns for categorizing information.

A husband comes home early because his wife had been looking haggard and tired lately. Instead of recognizing this as his way of expressing love, she filters it out. She says, "He just had nothing to do at the office. He knew that the boss would be there and wanted to get out of meeting with him. He is serving his own needs and doesn't want to work." A filter system can filter out any message in spite of the obvious meaning to others. There are many couples who, in their own language, are telling their spouses that they love them. But this sincere expression of love is discarded because it is filtered out.

When is the last time you told your husband that you loved him? What was his response? Did he hear you? Did you misinterpret his lack of response? Perhaps that meant, "I did not hear you" rather than meaning, "I do not care." Too often we assume that a statement is made followed by a straight-forward response to that statement. A diagram of the process that actually occurs would look like this:

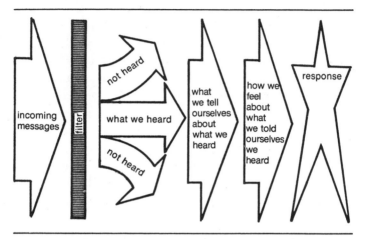

The husband, with a mother who always demanded of him and seldom supported him, will soon after the "I dos" not hear his wife's requests. The little girl whose busy father reassured her once a week between business trips that he really loved her with words such as, "It's just that the family has to eat," will soon discard the verbal reassurances uttered by her newly-wed husband.

I have noticed many couples enter a marriage without much awareness of themselves. What is it that they don't hear? Where are their blind spots? What language do they have difficulty understanding? What have they learned so efficiently to discard as rubbish because of their background?

Perhaps you would like to pause a minute and reflect

for yourself, "What do I filter out? What language do I understand best?" And if you are really feeling brave, ask your spouse. The appendices might help you do this.

Granted, some of the filtering is related to role differences. We were recently discussing at the dinner table this very area of communication with a young couple we enjoy because of their openness. Carol found she could understand how efforts to tell our spouses we love them are sometimes not heard. She related how she often tried to show George she loved him by religiously fulfilling her wifely duties of keeping the house clean. He, recently, not thinking in those terms, had come tramping with muddy feet through the living room having just won the victory over the clogged drain in the garage. Do you think he commented on the clean house —or even noticed it? He was still elated over his great prowess as a Roto-Rooter man. Carol, in turn, felt hurt because George simply ignored her efforts at expressing her love for him. In fact, he had written muddy footprints all over her message. Now she had a whole new set of feelings to deal with since she felt her message was rejected.

As mentioned in chapter one, most people are only able to understand those languages which they themselves speak. They assume everyone else will also understand these languages. This is, as we have seen throughout this book, a very dangerous assumption to make.

Remember that no matter what you think you have communicated, it may never have been heard. Because your spouse does not respond to your language don't jump to the conclusion that he or she has rejected your love. It may mean, "I filtered it" not, "I rejected it."

Principle 2: Learn to Speak Your Spouse's Language

"Marital happiness does not occur by chance. A happy husband and wife are happy because of what their partner says or does."[1] Fi uoy era gniog ot etacinummoc na edutitta fo evol drawot ruoy esuops, you must learn to speak his or her language. Of all the principles this is possibly the most crucial.

The golden rule now takes on a more subtle but more important meaning. It is not just that you do unto others as you would have others do unto you. Matthew 7:12 is not saying that you behave toward your spouse only as you want him or her to behave toward you. It is saying in essence seek to understand and meet the unique needs of others just as you want your unique needs understood and met.

What language does your spouse speak? Do you really know what he or she can understand? You might want to reflect for a few minutes on those times your spouse felt loved by you. In an experiment conducted by the Oregon Research Institute, a husband was told to double his affectionate behavior toward his wife. A week later when asked about her husband's increase in affection, the wife looked blankly at the researcher. The husband had increased his affection by taking time to wash the car—which was his language. She had not heard one peep of affection from him because that was not at all her language.[2]

Too often we want our spouses to switch to our language so we can communicate effectively. But this is not the way to develop communication. Let me say it again. If you want to communicate love to your mate, you must learn his or her languages.

In cases where there is already much tension or antagonism between marriage partners, the need to learn to speak the spouse's language is even more critical. When the wife tries to communicate affection, happiness or playfulness, the husband may well interpret this negatively. Dissatisfaction is increased.

When determining what language your spouse speaks, remember that he or she may speak several languages. It would be presumptuous to latch onto the first one that comes to mind without continuing to explore other possibilities. (To assist with this, I have included a series of questions in appendix B.) Once you have determined the language, then start your linguistic classes. Begin to learn how to speak his or her language effectively and precisely, or even several languages. When you first attempt to communicate you may not be a pro. Don't let this bother you. No one would expect you to be one. But just using a language is the best way to learn it. You begin behaving in ways that your mate can relate to, and these behaviors become more and more a part of your lifestyle.

If your wife feels loved when you help with the dishes, then roll up your sleeves and reach for Joy (the detergent as well as the feeling). If your husband feels loved when you meet his emotional needs, then find out what those are and begin to help fulfill them. Your spouse will never get the message if your expression toward him or her is the language that's meaningful only to you.

76

Principle 3: Find the Primary Language

Although most people have several languages which they can hear, it is imperative to find the primary language. If you eliminate their primary language from your repertoire, the others may be difficult for them to hear. Occasionally the lack of the key language may not only hamper the hearing and feeling of love, it may even eliminate it altogether. Its absence somehow disturbs emotional audio acuity so that little seems to reach the spouse. It is as though that primary language is the key to the acceptance of love on his or her part. The primary language opens the door to secondary languages. Its effective use is a necessary step before the others can be heard.

It is almost as if the husband says, "I can't accept language A, B or C unless you also speak D. However, if you speak D, I can also accept A, B and C."

For example, Harry's primary language is that of being helped. Mary may tell him she loves him, be understanding and spend time with him. But he does not hear her total message of love until she supports him with this key language. When Mary discovers this, Harry will be more open to hearing his secondary love language as well. He can feel loved when Mary tells him she loves him, as long as she has been helping him too.

What is the key language your spouse speaks? Is there one language which if left out would disrupt his or her ability to hear your messages? If you ranked them in terms of importance to your mate, what would you place at the top of the list? You might want to try that now by using appendix A and then compare your ranking with the ranking your mate gives.

Principle 4: Do Not Abuse the Primary Language

What happens when you reverse the languages of love and use them to communicate negative feelings? Margaret places primary importance on the verbal expressions of love from her husband. Once in a moment of anger Jonathan said that he didn't love her—that he even hated her. She was devastated. She was far more crushed than the wife with a different primary language. He had hit her in the point of greatest need and vulnerability. Had he expressed his anger differently by refusing to help her or by not defending her, she would have felt the anger but would not have been as greatly affected by it.

The primary language is the one that needs to be treated with the greatest respect. It should never be abused in arguments. Rather, it should be protected and sheltered from misuse. With the primary language you are talking through the channel that leads to the center of the person. Should it be abused, the person may well begin to close up the channel for defense. After closing off something as important as this, it would be difficult to open up again.

This principle alone should encourage mates to seek to understand the primary language of the other. If you simply did not want to inflict pain on your spouse thoughtlessly, you would do well to know where she or he is most vulnerable. This can prevent much hurt.

**Principle 5: Remember a Partial Language
May Be Heard in Reverse**

Whenever you set out to communicate affection, be sure

you complete the action. Partial actions may not carry the message you think they do and in fact may carry a message that is the opposite of what you are trying to communicate.

In our marriage Nan envisioned her role as taking care of the house and my role as taking care of the yard. Both of these were fairly traditional patterns in our homes as we grew up. In the last few years she has ventured into the area of gardening and found that she really enjoys it. While busy with the flowers she became more aware of how my involvement with work at the office caused the yard work to suffer. She decided, in love, that she would do me a favor and exercise the gift and language of helping. So she pruned many limbs of the shrubs around the yard and felt that I would surely appreciate her great kindness and help.

When Saturday came, however, and I walked into the back yard to find dry, brittle, thorny limbs strewn from one side of the yard to the other, I did not exactly feel loved. My reaction was, "Why did Nan make such a mess? Doesn't she realize I already have all I can do to keep the yard clean and the grass trimmed?" Needless to say, she didn't find me delighted at her communication because I didn't understand until later what she was trying to say. She saw my role as gardener and felt I would surely appreciate any little help I could get. Had she completed her task and picked up the trimmed branches, my initial reaction would have been much different.

Be sure your language is complete so your spouse can hear what you are saying. A partially communicated message may be worse than no message at all.

Principle 6: Eliminate the Negative
Admittedly, many marriages have many rough spots to work out. Learning how to communicate love does not automatically eliminate the negative. After you have begun speaking your mate's language effectively, there is yet one other consideration: How many negative feelings are you still introducing into your marriage? Are you expressing love but at the same time coming home to your wife with a critical approach? Or are you greeting your husband at the door like an emotional porcupine, wondering why he does not usually take you passionately into his arms?

Communicating negative and communicating affectionate feelings do not appear to be linked so that as one increases the other automatically decreases. They are not like a balance scale in which one side goes up and the other goes down proportionately. Therefore, it is also very useful to work at decreasing negative interactions while being sensitive to increasing positive feelings. According to some research, the decrease in the negative is just as important, if not more important, to marital satisfaction as increasing the positive.[3] At the same time I am not encouraging couples to totally eliminate communication of hurt or even of anger. Negative responses are the way a feeling is communicated, but not the content itself. One can and should honestly share a hurt without tearing down one's spouse's character or value.

There are several good reasons for eliminating the negative. First, the presence of negative messages can deter your spouse from being able to listen to positive messages. You do not want to destroy the very system you have set out to construct.

Second, as a friend of mine puts it, "You get good at what you practice." If you practice expressing lots of critical and hostile feelings, you will become good at it. All of us have seen people who have practiced criticism so much that they could make the starting line-up on an all-star team should they ever make negativism a professional sport.

Third, what we express to others comes back to us in response. This is often called the principle of reciprocation. Although affectionate behavior will be returned to us, so will negative behavior. But adverse behaviors are more likely to be reciprocated than positive behaviors. People are more predisposed to getting even when their feelings are hurt than when they are treated with kindness.

We all have attitudes of discord or rejection at times. Therefore, it is important not to practice using them in the marriage. Doing so brings familiarity and reciprocation.

11
Responsiveness

"How can I get my husband to begin to behave in a loving way?" "My wife is just not responsive." "I feel my needs as a person are not being met in my marriage. I'm just withering away with age." "Isn't there something I can do to enhance our communication of affectionate attitudes?"

Well, there are several things that can be done rather than sitting by helplessly. Just feeling as if you can do nothing is depressing in itself. So the first thing is to recognize that you can do something. Prayer is a good place to begin. And as in many other matters, I believe the Lord will guide you into what you can do next.

He might encourage you to be open and honest with your spouse. If so, go to him or her not with the idea of changing your spouse but with the idea of communicating your impressions, feelings, needs and your language. It is important that you not berate or chastise your mate for his or her shortcomings, but rather that you express *yourself*. Be careful not to put your spouse on the defensive. Therefore, talk about you. Don't talk to your mate about him or her. Start your sentences with "I," "I feel" or "I think" not with "You never" or "You always." The approach in both attitude and wording is very important. This opens the way for honest discussion.

Ridicule or Reward?
Understanding the principles of reinforcement can be a good next step. Although many factors affect our behavior, behavior that is rewarded (positive reinforcement) will often tend to increase and any behavior that is ignored or ridiculed (negative reinforcement) will often tend to decrease or stop entirely.

For example, a wife bakes an apple pie for dessert when guests come to dinner. When served, all graciously eat their pie but make no comments. The next time guests are invited, chocolate cake is served, and it creates quite a stir. The guests rave about the cake, and one or two ask for the recipe. When considering the next dinner party, guess what the dessert will be? The behavior, baking the chocolate cake, was reinforced or rewarded by praise. If the experience is repeated soon, cake will be served frequently at dinners.

This same principle applies to the particular language of love you enjoy hearing. Whenever your spouse helps in some way, tells you he or she loves you or gives you a big hug, reinforce it. Tell your mate you appreciate it, and let him or her know it means much to you. If your husband helps you with the dishes, fix him a cup of coffee.

"O.K., I get the idea. If my spouse is already expressing love in a language I really like to hear, I can reinforce it. But what if he is doing nothing? He never helps. He never tells me he loves me. He never hugs me."

In these situations one must start where the person is and build toward the goal. If you wait until your husband does the dishes to reinforce it, you may wait until Judgment Day, and then he won't have to do them anyway! So in beginning where he is, you find one little thing he has done, like put his dishes in the sink, and reinforce that behavior. As the behavior increases he may one day rinse off the dishes. Then reinforce that behavior. Or after he does a little job you asked him to do, make sure he knows he is thanked.

Is It a Bribe?

One of the first questions I usually get (with raised eyebrows) when this topic comes up concerns manipulation. Is it right to reward? Won't your husband always expect coffee? Isn't that exploiting or even bribery?

All behavior is affected by some kind of motivation and has some reinforcement either positive or negative. If your husband does the dishes, you are going to reinforce him positively or negatively no matter what you do. You cannot avoid it. So it may as well be done positively For even if you say nothing at all, he won't feel thanked Or he might wonder if he did it all wrong. If you look pleased, you have positively reinforced his behavior. It is worth noting that you cannot make a person do something he or she does not want to do. However, if doing the dishes becomes a rewarding experience because it is meaningful to you, your husband may want to do them.

Likewise I do not feel we could define this as bribery. Webster says a bribe has to do with a payoff in advance for illegal or wrong behavior. By contrast, reinforcement does not work well unless it comes after a behavior has been performed. Also, reinforcement usually is not related to illegal behavior. Again, if we do not respond, we extinguish the very language of love we want.

When I think of rewards I think of what Christ said about them. He assures us that the righteous will be rewarded. He presents the parable of the faithful steward who is rewarded. We are told there will be rewards of jewels in our crowns awaiting us in heaven. He does not seem to feel this is manipulating our behavior on this earth.

If you really enjoy one language and want it increased, there is something you can do. Express your feelings to your spouse and respond every chance you can.

12
"Hang Tough, Pardner"

A couple of summers ago we spent our vacation in Colorado. In the little town of Telluride, which sits up against the mountains in a box canyon, is a drugstore with one of those authentic, old soda fountains. I was in a booth in the back of the store enjoying a coke when my eyes caught sight of a greeting card on a nearby rack. On the outside of the card was a picture of an old Colorado cowboy. He was homely. Not that all Colorado cowboys are homely, but he was homely. His leathery face was penetrated by a white, whiskery stubble which was particularly noticeable on his protruding jaw. His shirt was spotted with dirt and grease and tobacco stains. The brim of his worn hat was stained with sweat. His face wore a gentle smile contrasting with his weathered face. As I opened the card and looked inside it read, "Hang tough, pardner."

A Deadly Inoculation

In our society we have grown accustomed to comfort. We have inoculated ourselves with the philosophy, "If it feels good, do it." This, of course, includes, "If it doesn't feel good, forget it." We have learned to pursue pleasure and comfort. We have learned to avoid anything that requires the mere idea of endurance. The world we live in is abundant with examples of taking the easy way out. Skyrocketing divorce rates, increased crime, school dropouts . . . all an indication of the philosophy of the day. Toffler argues in *Future Shock* that now we are a throwaway society, whether talking about paper plates and plastic forks or marriages.

Once we have developed a philosophy, consciously or not, it permeates every aspect of our lives. Today very few want to "hang tough" in their marriage. Of those who do, some do so because of a sense of purpose and some because they feel too guilty to let go. This is not a principle of being masochistic or staying in a painful situation to be a martyr but of enduring hardships for a cause that matters. Too often we scrap the cause in favor of the comfort.

The Bible, however, teaches toughness with patience. Undoubtedly the greatest example of this has been the love of God toward us. We are told that while we were in a state of sinfulness, rejecting God, he loved us so much he gave the most valuable asset he had, his Son, to redeem us from our condition. He expressed this indescribable love to us while we were rejecting him, not while we were loving him. The Bible tells us that we can have eternal life by accepting this gift of love. With patience God has spoken to mankind in his own language of love. Now it is up to each person to accept or reject that expression of love. We are not forced to hear God. He has chosen to express himself without any assurance from us that we will listen. He gives us his message, and we are to choose.

Floods Cannot Drown It

The Bible describes for us the strength and toughness of true love. We get a very different concept than the flightiness concept portrayed by the media.

> *Set me as a seal upon your heart,*
> *as a seal upon your arm;*
> *for love is strong as death,*
> *jealousy is cruel as the grave.*
> *Its flashes are flashes of fire,*
> *a most vehement flame.*
> *Many waters cannot quench love,*
> *neither can floods drown it.*
> *If a man offered for love*
> *all the wealth of his house,*
> *it would be utterly scorned. (Song 8:6-7)*

True love is stronger than the grave. It cannot even be quenched by death. Certainly we have seen instances of this. We are told that its coals are a vehement flame. Some theologians say this depicts the melting-together aspect of love, the characteristic that brings unity. Then we are told that even floods cannot drown love. True love is a force that is not done away with easily but one that endures and persists. This depicts a very different picture of love than we see in the world today.

When you can express love but do not feel as though it is well received, express it again and again. When you get to the point where you cannot comfortably go on expressing love, you "hang tough" and do it again.

That cowboy on the front of the card looked as though he could have endured an entire winter without shelter or food and still come out smiling. He didn't get that way overnight. He began a day at a time by facing and accepting a small hardship and seeing it through rather than backing away because he was tired or uncomfortable. He was soon able to toughen himself so that he could face situations which were even more uncomfortable.

How much time do we spend toughening ourselves? I am not talking about shutting out our emotions. I am talking about enduring that which we dislike. We can err in two directions. We can be too closed from feeling and repress everything, or we can be too demanding that everything go our way. More often I have seen Christians who are not tough enough. The minute something does not go their way, they flare up and then give up. They come into marriage looking for a place to be loved rather than a place to love. If we communicate love and sense that our spouse does not hear, we say it again. True love does not demand to be heard.

Recently at the wedding of a young couple I had come to appreciate, the minister described love from 1 Corinthians 13:4-7.

Love is patient and kind; love is not jealous or boastful; it is not arrogant or rude. Love does not insist on its own way; it is not irritable or resentful; it does not rejoice at wrong, but rejoices in the right. Love bears all things, believes all

90

things, hopes all things, endures all things.
"Love bears all things, believes all things, hopes all things, endures all things." There it was, the characteristic of love we need today. I am not sure the couple truly heard it during the ceremony, but they will need it throughout their lives as they build their marriage together.

"A new commandment I give to you, that you love one another" (Jn. 13:34).

Appendix A: Ranking Languages

(Note: Both appendices A and B can help you and your spouse determine what languages you understand best. Appendix A should be completed first. In this way what you think *are your key languages [the results of appendix A] can be compared to a possibly more revealing picture in appendix B.)*

	Wife's Ratings		Husband's Ratings	
	Mine	Husband's	Mine	Wife's
1. Meeting Material Needs	____	____	____	____
2. Helping	____	____	____	____
3. Spending Time Together	____	____	____	____
4. Meeting Emotional Needs	____	____	____	____
5. Saying It with Words	____	____	____	____
6. Saying It with Touch	____	____	____	____
7. Being on the Same Side	____	____	____	____
8. Bringing Out the Best	____	____	____	____

Step 1. Wife rates her languages 1 through 8, starting with the most important.

Step 2. She then rates her husband's languages.

Step 3. Husband follows same procedure, covering up his wife's rankings.

Step 4. Compare and discuss.

Appendix B: Language Inventory

On a piece of paper complete each sentence. You may be able to do so in more than one way. If possible, have your spouse do the same on a separate sheet.

1. During childhood I knew that my parents loved me because they . . .

2. During our courtship. three of the characteristics that attracted me to my husband/wife were . . .

3. The three times in our marriage that I have felt the closest to my spouse were when he/she . . .

4. When down and in need of support, I like my husband wife to . . .

5. One of the things I like best about my husband/wife is that he/she . . .

6. After an argument I feel reunited when my husband wife . . .

7. I gain a sense of inner comfort and warmth when my husband/wife . . .

8. I feel romantic when my husband/wife . . .

9. One thing that my husband/wife contributed to our relationship, enriching it, is . . .

10. I want to pursue growth in our relationship because my husband/wife . . .

11. In our relationship, I emotionally need my husband/wife to . . .

12. I well up with strong affectionate feelings when my husband/wife . . .

13. I wish my husband/wife would more frequently . . .

14. It hurts my feelings most when my husband/wife does not . . .

15. I feel a sense of acceptance and worth when my husband/wife . . .

16. If I wanted to feel loved, my first impulse would be to ask my spouse to . . .

17. If I wanted to increase our marital happiness I would ask my husband/wife to . . .

18. The nicest gift I ever received from my husband/wife was when . . .

19. I feel God loves me because . . .

20. In the past when I greatly wanted to show my love for my spouse I . . .

21. The most meaningful thing a husband/wife could do for their spouse is . . .

Once you have finished, each of you should mark beside each response the number of the language (see list below) which best describes that response. Add the total to determine which are the languages you marked most frequently. These should help indicate which languages you are most fluent in. Discuss your results with each other.

1. Meeting Material Needs   5. Saying It with Words
2. Helping   6. Saying It with Touch
3. Spending Time Together   7. Being on the Same Side
4. Meeting Emotional Needs   8. Bringing Out the Best

Notes

Chapter One

[1]Eric S. Strauss, "Couples in Love," Clinical Psychology (1974), 2450.

[2]Tom Wills, Robert Weiss, Gerald Patterson, "A Behavior Analysis of the Determinants of Marital Satisfaction," Journal of Consulting and Clinical Psychology 42, No. 6 (1974), 810.

[3]Clark, Boyd, Kempler, Johannet, Leonard, McPherson, "Teaching Interpersonal Communications to Troubled Families," Family Process 13, No. 3 (1974), 325.

Chapter Two

[1]Dwight Small, After You've Said I Do (Old Tappan, New Jersey: Fleming H. Revell, 1968), p. 236.

Chapter Four

[1]David Knox, Marriage Happiness (Champaign, Illinois: Research Press, 1974), p. 19.

Chapter Five

[1]Bernard L. Greene, A Clinical Approach to Marital Problems (Springfield, Illinois: Charles C. Thomas, 1970), p. 45.

[2]Paul Tournier, To Understand Each Other (Atlanta Georgia: John Knox Press, 1967), p. 40.

[3]Ibid., p. 9.

[4]Small, p. 82.

[5]Ibid., p. 92.

[6]James D. Mallory, The Kink and I (Wheaton, Illinois: Victor Books, 1973), p. 146.

[7]Tournier, p. 25.

[8]C. S. Lewis, The Four Loves (New York: Harcourt Brace Jovanovich, 1960), p. 168.

Chapter Seven
[1]*Allen Fromme as quoted by Small, p. 221.*
[2]*Elton Trueblood as quoted by Small, ibid.*

Chapter Nine
[1]*John Powell,* Why Am I Afraid to Tell You Who I Am? *(Niles, Illinois: Argus Communications, 1969), p. 43.*
[2]*Strauss, 2450 B.*

Chapter Ten
[1]*Knox, p. 3.*
[2]*Wills, Weiss, Patterson, 810.*
[3]*Ibid., 809.*